DIARY
OF A
MINECRAFT
ZOMBIE

Book 5

Zack Zombie

Sunday

I can't believe it!

It's almost here.

Just a few more weeks till summer break, which means no more Scare school!

That means no more teachers, no more books, no more villagers' dirty looks...

And no more having to go out and scare villagers for an entire summer.

Now, don't get me wrong. I like scaring the occasional villager.

Especially when they drop cool stuff like cake, or a bow and arrow, or something like that.

But nothing beats being able to do whatever you want on summer vacation.

Now, I was trying to think about what I'm going to do for summer vacation.

I was thinking of just playing video games and eating cake all day, and doing it every day for the next three months.

But, I'm sure my Mom and Dad are not going to let me have that much fun.

They seem to think that ruining my summer vacation is part of their Zombie parent job description or something.

Or I was thinking of just spending my whole summer hanging out with Skelee, Slimey, and Creepy, and getting into all kinds of trouble.

But there's not a lot of trouble we can get into in a small town like the one we live in.

Maybe we can tip over a few spiders, or knock on the witch's door and run away.

But after the first day, we're going to have to find out what to do with the rest of the summer.

My Mom and Dad said they were thinking of sending me to camp for the summer.

But there's no way I'm going to spend part of my summer making crafts and eating gross camp food.

Plus, I would probably miss all my friends, Sally, and Steve.

I just have to make sure that I get a good report card so my parents don't punish me by sending me to camp.

Well, anyway, all I know is that I can't wait for school to finish.

All I have to do is get through these next few weeks and I'm home free!

Monday

A lot of the kids at school today were talking about what they're going to do this summer.

Skelee said that his parents were to going to take him to Yellowbone National Park. I think he said that's where his parents are from.

Slimey said he was going to the Superflat Biome. He said they have big fields where he can have fun and jump around.

And Creepy said his parents were sending him away to camp.

I felt really bad for Creepy. But he said he's been going to camp for the past three years.

He said he liked camp because they make crafts, play lots of sports, and eat really good food.

Sometimes I think Creepy is living in another world…

The guys asked me what I was doing for summer.

I just told them I was going to play video games and eat cake all summer.

"I wish I could do that," Skelee said. "But my parents always ruin it. I think they feel like if they let me have fun, then they're not being good skeleton parents or something."

I'm really going to miss my friends for the summer.

But I think Steve is going to be around so I'll hang out with him.

I went to go visit Steve to see what he was up to.

I found him night fishing by the lake.

"Hey Steve!" I said.

"AAAAAHHH!"

"Zombie, why do you always sneak up on me like that?!!"

"I've been practicing for my Scare class exam that's coming up in a few weeks," I said.

"Oh, that makes sense," Steve said.

"By the way," Steve said, "I was just thinking of something I wanted to ask you. Why did your parents name you Zombie? Why didn't they call you 'Joe' or 'Edgar' or something like that?"

"Zombie is not my real name. That's just a nickname people call me," I said. "My real name is Zack. Zack Zombie."

"Zack Zombie, really?"

"Yeah, most Zombies have the last name Zombie," I said.

Like my uncle Harry Zombie or my neighbor Seymour Zombie.

There are a few kids at school with the name Zombie too. There's:

Ima Zombie,

Ada Zombie,

Major Zombie,

Nada Zombie,

Norma Lee Zombie,

Sacha Zombie,

Ivana Zombie,

So Yung Zombie (I think he's Korean),

Zeena Zombie,

Yuri Zombie,

And there's even a kid named Zombie Zombie.

"Oh, so Zombie is kind of like Smith or Jones with humans," Steve said.

"I guess," I said. "Is your last name Smith?"

"No… Actually, I don't know my last name."

"Whoa," I said. "But I bet if you did it would be something cool like 'Steve Human' or something like that."

Steve just looked at me… Confused.

Tuesday

Tomorrow is picture day.

That's when we take pictures for our school yearbook.

I don't like taking pictures.

No matter how I smile, I always end up looking like a real noob.

10

Big mouth Jeff always looks really good in his pictures.

And this year he got lucky. He got a case of the chicken pox right before picture day.

Now, he's going to look really awesome.

A lot of the other kids got chicken pox too.

But for some reason I couldn't catch it.

It's like all the other kids get all the cool diseases like: measles, mumps, chicken pox, small pox, and even some cool flesh-eating diseases too.

But for some reason, I can't get any.

It's like the only disease I ever catch is a case of bad luck.

Wednesday

My Mom got me a new outfit for picture day today.

It's a good thing that picture day is only once a year.

I think I look like a real dork.

When I got to school all the kids were dressed in their best clothes.

I had never seen mobs look so good.

And then big mouth Jeff and his crew arrived, all covered in chicken pox… And they looked awesome.

I wanted to look awesome.

So I decided to fake the measles.

Hey, I couldn't get the chicken pox, but I think I could fake the measles.

So, I took a red marker from my teacher's desk and I ran to the bathroom.

But the bathroom was full of mob kids getting ready for pictures.

So I ran to the janitor's closet instead.

There was no mirror in there so I just started dotting my face with the marker.

"Man, this is gonna' look so good," I thought.

Once I was finished, I walked out of the janitor's closet.

I was so proud of my measles that I decided to strut down the hall so that everyone could see me.

All of a sudden, all the kids started staring at me, and giggling.

Some kids even started laughing out loud.

I caught my reflection in the window, and I had accidentally dotted my face with a black marker, instead of a red one.

I knew it was weird that the marker cap was red, and the rest of it was black.

My face looked like a green and black checkerboard.

I ran to the bathroom to wash it off, but the bathroom was still full.

So I ran back to the janitor's closet again.

Just my luck, when I tried to use the sink, it was broken.

Then I saw a big bottle of something that had liquid in it.

It had an old label that was really hard to read. I think said, "BLE-CH."

It sounded like something you'd use if you felt like your face looked "Blech."

So I soaked a rag in it and rubbed my face over and over again. I had to rub really hard to get the marker off because it was permanent.

It was weird because by the time I finished the rag was full of all kinds of colors including black, green, and red.

But I was just glad I got it off.

So, I walked outside and did my strut down the hallway.

This time, no one was laughing, but they sure were staring at me with the biggest eye sockets I had ever seen.

"Man, I must look real good," I thought.

I walked into the room where they were taking pictures, and the photographer's eye sockets grew really big too.

16

"Are you sure you want to take your picture?" he asked.

I guess he thought I missed a button on my shirt or something.

"Go for it!" I said proudly.

"OK," he said with a weird look on his face. Then he took my picture.

Man, I can't wait till the yearbook comes out.

This picture is going to look so awesome!

Thursday

Stayed home from school to grow my face back today.

Ouch...

My Mom said it was probably the flash from the camera that made my face melt off like that.

"I guess my baby is just a sensitive soul," she said.

Oh brother...

Friday

Today at school, we had to write an essay about what we are going to do for the summer.

I was going to write about how I was going to stay home all summer and play video games and eat cake.

But I didn't want my teacher to tell my Mom and Dad at the Parent-Teacher conference tonight.

I don't like Parent-Teacher conferences.

I think teachers and parents probably get together to plot ways to ruin all the kids' summer.

I can imagine the Principal getting up and saying, "OK everyone. How can we make sure we ruin the kids' summer this year?"

"Make sure they have lots of chores to do!" somebody would say.

"Make sure you invite all of your weird relatives to stay with you for the summer… And make sure you give them the kid's room to sleep in," another person would say.

And of course somebody is going to say, "Send them away to camp for the whole summer, where they can make crafts and eat nasty camp food."

That's probably the one idea that everybody is going to agree with.

Then I realized that if I just write my essay about "how much I love camp," instead of my video game and cake marathon, then my teacher won't have anything to say to

20

my parents at the Parent-Teacher conference tonight.

It was genius!

So I wrote my whole essay on how cool it would be to go to camp for the summer.

I wrote about much I love to make crafts, especially lanyards and macaroni pictures.

I wrote about how great the cafeteria food is.

I even wrote about how camp would be a great way for me to make new friends for the summer.

I'm sure with an essay like that, my teacher will be totally fooled and not tell my parents about my real summer plans.

I got this in the bag!

21

Saturday

My life is ruined!

My parents came home last night talking about how the teacher showed them the great essay I wrote.

"I never knew you liked camp so much, son," Dad said.

"Yes, Honey. We were going to give you the summer to do whatever you wanted," my Mom said. "Now that we know you love camp so much, we signed you up to go to camp this summer. There was a camp representative at the Parent-Teacher conference last night, so we signed you up right away."

"We even put down a non-refundable deposit for it too, son," Dad said. "So, congratulations, you're going to camp!"

OMZ!

My life is totally ruined!

Now I'm going to spend my summer in the Swamp Biome at camp.

Oh man, this is terrible!

What am I going to do?!!

I decided to ask Steve some advice on how to get out of my terrible situation.

I found Steve in a cave crafting some fireworks.

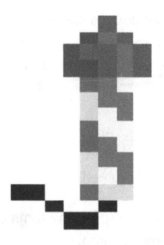

All of a sudden, "BOOOOMMM!"

All that was left of him were his tools and his weapons.

A few minutes later, Steve walked into the cave behind me.

I totally understand how he does that trick now.

"Hey, Steve!"

"Wassup, Zombie?" Steve said.

"I have a question for you."

"Shoot!" Steve said.

So, I picked up his bow and arrow and I shot him.

"Ow! What'd you do that for?"

"You told me to shoot," I said.

"Forget about it. What's your question?"

"My Mom and Dad are making me go to camp this summer," I said. "But I don't want to go. I've got to find a way out of it, and I need your help."

"Why are they sending you to camp?" Steve asked.

"Well, I kind of told them I wanted to go."

25

"And now, you don't want to go?" Steve asked.

"No, I never wanted to go," I said.

Steve just looked at me… Confused.

"Well, I thought if I wrote an essay about how much I wanted to go to camp, my Mom and Dad wouldn't send me to camp," I said.

After I said it out loud, I realized how dumb that idea was.

"It sure made sense at the time," I said.

"So, you want to get out of camp, but your parents think you really want to go?" Steve asked.

"Yeah."

"Well, you could always get in trouble and they'll punish you by taking away your summer camp," Steve said.

26

Man, Steve is so smart. That was the best idea I have ever heard.

So, I've got to get in trouble so that my parents will punish me by taking camp away.

I can do that. I just have to find a class that I can fail this semester, and they'll punish me for sure if that happens.

See, this is why I always go to Steve when I need some good advice.

Sunday

So I figured out what I'm going to do.

The Annual School Science Fair is supposed to be this week.

Everybody in my science class is supposed to bring a project.

And my Mom and Dad have been reminding me about it all semester.

So I was thinking, if I make the worst science project ever, then I'll flunk my science class for sure.

Then my parents will ground me and not let me go to camp.

So, I need to come up with the worst science experiment ever.

Let me see...

I could enter my booger collection.

Naw, I did that last year and I still passed my class.

Or I could enter one of my smelly gym socks. There's a lot of science going on there.

Naw. Knowing my science teacher, he'll probably give me an "A" for creativity or something.

Or, I could dissect my little brother and show that little brothers are really rotten to the core.

Nah. Even though it would be a lot of fun, I would probably have a hard time holding him down.

No. It's got to be the worst science experiment ever known to Zombie-kind.

"I know! I'll enter Steve, a human being, as my science experiment," I thought.

Oh man, that'll get me a failing grade for sure.

Either that or it'll scare the daylights out of my science teacher and all of the other kids. Then I'll really get in a lot of trouble.

Wow, summer vacation here I come!

Monday

I told Steve about my plans for the science fair and he was all in.

"So, I'm going to stick some electrodes to your forehead and neck. Then, I'm going to throw a switch, and you're going to come to life," I said.

"You mean like Frankenstein?" Steve asked.

"Franken-who?"

"Frankenstein... You know, the mad-scientist that collected body parts and sowed them together. Then he shocked the body full of lightning and it came to life," Steve said.

"Never heard of him," I said. "But, anyway, the science fair is on Wednesday. You just have to meet me before school, outside of the gym, and I'll let you in through the back. Got it?"

"Got it," Steve said.

This idea is sure to give me a flunking grade.

Then I'll be free from my trip to "prison camp," and I'll be able to enjoy my summer.

This was a really great idea, I thought.

Wow, I never knew I was so smart.

Yeah me.

Tuesday

Today, Creepy was telling me all about how excited he was about going to camp.

He told me that they were going to have a big talent show this year, and he was going to be part of a band.

"I didn't know you could play an instrument," I said to Creepy.

"Yeah, I play a mean set of drums," Creepy said.

Now, I was going to ask him how he plays drums without arms, but I think some things are best left alone.

I told the guys my idea for the science fair.

"Whoa, that's really cool," they said.

The guys aren't very smart, so if they liked it, I'm sure that the teacher is going to hate my idea and flunk me.

Later, at home, I prepared my machine with electrodes and everything.

I took the extra car battery from the garage and connected it. It started sparking and making noise.

"MUAHAHAHAHA!!!" I said real loud.

I thought I might as well act the part and make it look real.

So, I was all set.

When I came down to dinner, my Mom and Dad asked me about the science fair.

"What are you going to do for your project this year?" Dad asked. "I hope you're not entering your booger collection again. I'm sorry, buddy, but a booger collection is not exactly science fair material. Especially since everyone has one."

"Don't worry, Dad. This year I went all out," I said. "My project is going to be a real winner."

"Honey, I'm so proud of you," Mom said. "And, if you win, we were thinking of giving you an extra week of camp as a reward."

"Yeah!" I said, knowing full well I was going to flunk miserably, and spend my summer playing video games and eating tons of cake.

Wednesday

They said that a famous Zombie was visiting the school and was going to help judge the science fair this year.

"That's great," I thought, "Now I know I'll definitely fail."

So I got everything ready, and I let Steve in through the back of the gym.

I had Steve lie down on a table and I put a blanket over him.

Then I rolled him out next to my electrode machine.

The famous visiting Zombie was really tall. Almost as tall as my friend Mutant.

He went around with the science teacher, judging all of the other science fair projects.

He didn't look too impressed though.

"Great, then he'll really hate mine," I thought.

My experiment was the last one to get judged.

So when the famous Zombie and the science teacher came to my table, I got into character.

"MUAHAHAHAHAHA!!!" I said, "Now I will bring this human back to life. MUAHAHAHAHAHA!!!"

I threw the switch and all of the lights went out in the gym.

My electrode machine was shooting sparks and lighting up the whole place.

"RISE, MY CREATURE! RISE!"

Suddenly, Steve sat up from the table.

"IT'S ALIVE! IT'S ALLLIIIIIIIVE!"

Steve stood up and he stretched his arms out like a Zombie and said, "UUURRGGHH!!!"

All of a sudden, the mob kids started running and screaming out of the gym. "IT'S A HUMAN!" they screamed, as Steve chased after them.

"Man, it's working," I thought. "This is a disaster. I'm going to flunk this class for sure."

"MUAHAHAHAHAHA!!!"

All of a sudden, the lights come back on.

The visiting famous Zombie was standing right in front of me.

As he ' stared at me, he did the weirdest thing ever.

He raised his big hand and wiped a tear from his eye.

"That was the most amazing thing I have ever seen!" he said. Then he ran out of the gym sobbing.

My science teacher came over to me and said, "Congratulations, Zombie. That was the most authentic reenactment of the creation of Frankenstein that I have ever seen. But how did you know that Frankenstein was going to visit today? I only heard about it this morning…"

I just looked at him... Confused.

Then I dreaded what he was going to say next.

"Everyone, Everyone! The winner of this year's science fair, for outstanding creativity, authenticity and imagination goes to Zack Zombie, for his project—The Rise of Frankenstein!"

Everybody in the gym started applauding and cheering.

"How do you feel, son?" my science teacher asked me.

"Great," I said, as I thought about my parents adding another week to my summer prison camp sentence.

Thursday

My parents took me to "The Woking Dead" Chinese restaurant to celebrate me winning the science fair.

"We're so proud of you, son," Dad said. "You're a chip off the old block."

"Maybe he can work with you at the Nuclear Waste Plant for the summer," Mom said. "That way he'll be able to develop his scientific talent."

I just tried to bury my sorrow in my Zombie egg roll.

"So, son," Dad said. "I just put another non-refundable deposit for another week at camp for you. I don't know how we're going to afford it. But you're worth it."

"Maybe we should send him to science camp too, this summer," Mom said.

I threw up my egg roll.

"Wow, look how excited he is," Mom said.

Friday

The good thing that came from winning the science fair is that Mom and Dad let me go to a sleepover at Skelee's house to celebrate.

So me, Slimey, and Creepy went over to Skelee's house for a sleepover movie night.

All of the guys congratulated me on my science fair win.

Then Creepy started talking more about how great it is that I'm going to camp for an extra week.

"There's going to be a competition against the camp next to us," Creepy said. "We've lost every year since I've been there. But with your science skills, I think we can really beat them this year."

"Guys, I don't want to talk about it anymore," I said. "What movie are we watching tonight, anyway?"

"Creepaway Camp 3: Terror in the Woods," Skelee said. "I heard it was really good."

Oh brother…

Saturday

I went back to Steve to ask more advice about how to get out of camp.

"Congratulations on your win," Steve said sarcastically.

I just looked at him, depressed.

"Now what am I going to do?" I said. "My Mom and Dad are going to give me two weeks at camp, and I don't know what to do."

"Don't worry. You still have plenty of time to mess things up," Steve said. "Don't you have any big exams coming up soon?"

"Yeah! I have a big Scare class exam on Monday. Hey, if I mess that up, then my parents will ground me for sure," I said.

45

"But the only problem," I said, "is that the exam is going to be graded on how well we can scare villagers. And villagers are real easy to scare. They're scared of everything."

"Well, if you make them laugh, then there's no way they can be scared," Steve said.

Wow. Steve is a genius. Where does he come up with this stuff?

"That's a great idea. But I'm going to have to come up with something to make them laugh," I said.

"I've got a great routine for you," Steve said. "Every time I do it, it always makes my friends laugh."

"Thanks, Steve. I really appreciate it."

So Steve showed me his routine and we practiced it for a few hours.

Man, I can't wait to do this routine on my Scare test on Monday.

I'm going to have those villagers in stitches.

Summer vacation, here I come!

Sunday

Today I spent the whole day practicing the comedy routine at home in front of a mirror.

I never thought of myself as a comedian.

I tried to tell a joke once.

It went like this…

"Why was the Zombie afraid to cross the road?

Because he lost his guts!"

I love that joke!

I don't know why, but every time I tell it, nobody laughs.

48

But I know since Steve came up with this routine, it's got to be funny.

The good thing is that there's not a lot of talking in this routine, just silly movements.

And I could tell while practicing in the mirror, that it's going to be really funny.

I can't wait to try it on the villagers tomorrow.

Monday

I woke up late today, so I had to rush out of bed and head out straight to school.

I didn't even get a chance to eat breakfast.

I didn't care because I was just so excited to mess up my scare exam, and get my life back this summer.

I made it to Ms. Bones' Scare class when she said, "Kids, remember, this exam will count toward 50% of your grade. So make sure you give it your all when you go out and scare those villagers today."

"Not me," I thought, "I'm going to get those villagers laughing so hard, they won't be scared at all."

50

When we got to the village, all the other kids picked a villager to scare.

And the other kids did really well.

But then it was my turn.

I picked a villager that I saw picking crops.

Steve also gave me some music to go with the routine, so I turned on the boom box and jumped out of the bushes.

"Everybody Dance Now!"

I started doing my routine, and it was good!

I was all up into my routine, when more and more villagers gathered around me.

I was really getting into it.

Soon, the entire village was gathered around me, and they were into it too.

"Hey guys, check out what Zombie is doing!" one of the mob kids yelled.

Then all of the mob kids jumped out of the bushes at once.

All of a sudden, the entire village went crazy and the villagers started running and screaming.

"It's the Zombie Apocalypse!" a villager yelled.

"AAAAHHHH!!!" was all I heard, as all of the villagers scattered to their homes.

Ms. Bones was shocked.

"You scared the entire village all at once!" she said. "That was the most amazing thing I have ever seen!"

Then she said, "You get an A plus for your scare test, and for the class. Congratulations, Zombie!"

Man, I really hate my life.

Tuesday

Today my parents took me to the "Drool and Gruel" diner to celebrate my A+ on my Scare exam.

"Son, you never stop surprising us," Dad said. "We talked to your teacher and she said that your reenactment of the Zombie Apocalypse was the best thing she had ever seen. You scared every villager in that town."

"Thanks Dad," I said as I buried my sorrow in a Drool Shake.

"Honey, tell him the surprise," Mom said.

"What surprise?"

"Well, son, Ms. Bones was so impressed with your work that she spoke to the Principal. And the Principal agreed to sponsor you for

54

an extra week of camp as a reward. Isn't that amazing?!!"

I threw up my Drool shake.

"Look how excited he is, honey. He can't even keep his Drool shake down," Mom said.

Life is so unfair.

Wednesday

Well, even though it's been a crazy few days, the one cool thing is that yearbooks come out today.

Man, I can't wait!

I've been looking forward to seeing my yearbook picture since we took our pictures.

I bet I'm going to look real good, too.

Maybe, I'll even look like an 8th grader!

I'm going to get everybody to sign my yearbook too.

They're probably going to write something like "The coolest Zombie in school," or,

"The Zombie most likely to succeed." Or something cool like that.

Mom said that yearbook pictures are great because it's a way that people can remember you for the rest of your life.

When she pulls out her yearbook I can tell it brings back really great memories for her... Even though it was a really, really, really long time ago.

Dad told me not to get my hopes up too high, though.

I think it's because my Dad's yearbook picture looks like he was one of the nerdiest kids in school.

"Your yearbook pictures are only a snapshot of a very short period of your life," he said. "You always outgrow those pictures anyway."

I don't know how much I believe that last thing he said.

57

Under his yearbook picture it said, "The most likely to work in a Nuclear Waste Plant."

I think I'm going to get extra pictures made to give out to people.

I'm going to get some for grandma.

I'm going to get a few for Sally.

And I'll probably need a few for my photo spread in ZQ magazine...

Thursday

OMZ!

My life is officially over.

As soon as I opened my yearbook I saw my picture...

I couldn't believe it.

I looked terrible!

My picture was so awful that all the kids in school were laughing at me when I walked down the hallway.

When I wasn't paying attention, somebody wrote in my yearbook, "The Zombie most likely to be mistaken for a human."

Somebody else wrote, "The Zombie most likely to work at the Chum Bucket."

And somebody even wrote, "The Zombie most likely to host American Idol."

When I got to class, Ms. Bones had all of the yearbook pictures scanned on her laptop.

So she had a giant picture of somebody in the class projected on the screen every few seconds, with a speech bubble asking the class a question.

When my picture came up, the question next to it said, "How scary am I?"

All of the mob kids burst out laughing.

It was the most embarrassing day ever.

Friday

I went to see Steve today.

Even though being a Scare School Zombie kid is really tough, it's really great to have a friend like Steve I can talk to.

"What's the matter, Zombie?" Steve asked. "You look really blue."

"Really? I'm usually a nice shade of green."

"No, I mean you look really sad," Steve said.

"Well, this is going to be the worst summer ever!" I said. "Not only are my parents going to send me to camp for three weeks, but I got my yearbook pictures back and they're the worst ever!"

"Really? Let me see," he said.

I gave him my yearbook and he took a look at it.

Then he burst out laughing.

"It's not funny, you know," I said.

"Sorry. I didn't mean to laugh. It's just that you look like a really famous person from where I'm from," Steve said.

"Really? He looks like that and he's famous?"

"Yeah, he's really popular too," he said. "But you're lucky. At least it's not as bad as my picture."

Steve showed me his yearbook picture.

"Whoa."

"Yeah, I like to make funny faces for my yearbook pictures," he said. "I just figured that if I can laugh at myself, then I really don't care if other people laugh at me either."

"But don't you care that this is the way people are going to remember you for the rest of your life?" I said.

"My real friends are going to remember me for more than my dumb yearbook picture," he said.

"Yeah, I guess you're right… You know, now that I look at it, my yearbook picture is kind of funny," I said.

And we both started laughing.

Man, every time I talk to Steve, I always feel better.

I don't know how I would've been able to get through my Zombie middle school life without a friend like him.

I just wish he could help me find a way out of going to camp.

Saturday

I had a "day-mare" today that my parents abandoned me at camp.

I walked into a room where some mob kids were quietly making some lanyards and macaroni pictures.

All of a sudden, the kids grabbed me and wrapped the lanyards around my neck.

Then another group of kids glued macaroni and googly eyes on my head in the shape of a smiley face.

I ran out of there and ran to the camp cafeteria to hide. Then, while I was there, the camp food suddenly came to life and attacked me.

66

I ran as fast as I could into a group of camp counselors.

"Help me, please," I said.

"Sure, we'll help you. We love helping ourselves to the kids at camp…"

Suddenly, all of the camp counselors turned human, and they started saying, "Braaaaiiiinnnss!"

They wanted to eat my brains!

So, I ran to the nurse's office to get help. The camp nurse pulled out a huge tongue depressor and said, "Open your mouth and say Ahhhh!"

Right before my eyes she turned into a rotten flesh eating witch that wanted to have me for lunch.

"Watch me open my mouth and say AHAHAHAHA!" she cackled, as her mouth opened up really big and she swallowed me whole!

Then I woke up.

"Oh man. I've got to find a way out of this camp situation," I thought.

If I don't, I'm going to be eaten by the camp counselors, the nurse, or the cafeteria lunch.

There's got to be a way that I can flunk out of a class and get my parents to punish me by taking camp away.

But the only thing I have left for the school year is my dumb presentation for mob history class.

The only problem is that it doesn't count that much toward my grade. So even if I skip it, I'll still pass the class.

But you know, we're supposed do our presentations in front of the whole school assembly.

And everybody, including the Principal and all of the parents are going to be there.

I bet if I make it the dumbest, craziest, and the most diabolical presentation ever, they're going to have to flunk me.

But it's got to be really bad. So bad that I might have to change schools after I do it.

Now I just have to come up with an idea for my presentation.

I bet you Steve will have a great idea!

Sunday

I met up with Steve and I told him my idea.

"You know, you can do a presentation about where Zombies come from," Steve said.

"Where do they come from?" I asked. "I've been trying to get my Mom to tell me but every time I bring it up, she keeps changing the subject."

"I've heard stories," Steve said. "Most of the stuff I know came from movies."

"Well, if there is one thing I know about movies, is that they're really accurate," I said.

So me and Steve spent the whole night putting my presentation together.

I even got the other guys to agree to help act out different parts in it.

Man, we added so much crazy stuff into the presentation that it'll probably get me banned from school.

Hey, a kid's gotta' do what he's gotta' do... Especially when summer vacation is on the line.

Monday

Well, today we're having our end of year assembly.

We're going to be showing our presentations to the whole 7th grade class, including all of the teachers, the Principal, and the parents.

My presentation is ready. And the guys are ready.

I think this presentation is going to go down in history as the most infamous presentation ever given at a Mob middle school.

I actually think that it could get me arrested.

But hey, as long as I don't have to go to camp, that's all that matters.

Here goes nothing...

Monday Night Special Entry

I think it worked!

When it was my turn to do my presentation, I could tell that people were looking forward to something like all the other kids did.

So I knew my presentation would have a good amount of shock value.

Before I started my presentation, they turned off all the lights, except for a spotlight on the stage.

I walked out onto the stage and I started telling the tale of the "Untold Story of the Origin of Zombies."

And it went like this:

Where do Zombies come from?

Not many people know.

But after some extensive investigative Zombie journalism, we've discovered the truth.

It all began when the human government decided that they wanted to create stronger soldiers.

They had lost too many battles, and now they wanted to win every war that they fought.

So they approached some soldiers in their army to join a special secret project.

The only requirement was that the soldiers they chose had no living relatives.

This way, no one could claim their bodies in case something went wrong.

75

So, they exposed these soldiers to an experimental virus to enhance their abilities and make them into super soldiers.

The experiment seemed to be working.

But then, something terrible happened...

The soldiers went crazy, and they were horribly disfigured.

Ultimately, the experiment claimed their lives.

But, when the soldiers were being prepared for burial, they suddenly came to life.

They were not only walking, but they had enhanced strength, enhanced sense of smell and enhanced hearing.

They attacked the soldiers in charge of burying them. And the recently bitten soldiers also transformed into the living dead.

Before long, the entire army base was contaminated with the virus.

Once everyone in the base was exposed, the virus mutated and the soldiers began having an overwhelming craving for something warm and mushy.

They longed for brains!

Soon, the army of the living dead found their way to the next unsuspecting town in search of brains.

They attacked that town, biting anything that moved both human and animal.

Soon that town was overrun.

The virus spread from town to town, and city to city, until the entire world was contaminated.

It was the first Zombie Apocalypse.

After hundreds of years had passed, the Zombies started to evolve and began developing intelligent thoughts.

They began forming villages, and then towns, and then entire cities of Zombies were created.

The Zombies made great advances in health and science, and became highly advanced technologically.

But, eventually the Zombies' appetite for brains and warm flesh gave way to an even greater craving...

The craving for CAKE!

Their overwhelming desire for cake resulted in an explosive rise in the baking industry.

Cake shops began springing up on every corner of every Zombie city street.

They just couldn't get enough!

The human race began growing again, too.

Human villages of farmers and miners began springing up.

And because the Zombies were a peaceful race, they coexisted with the humans by staying away from them.

But soon, the Zombie's resources began to become scarce, especially the cake.

So Zombies began scaring villagers in order to get the supplies they needed, especially the highly valued resource of cake.

Now Zombies send their kids to Scare School to train their children from a very young age.

They train them on how to effectively scare humans in order to get their needed supplies, especially cake.

And so it has been until today.

Thank you.

The entire audience was dead quiet.

Everyone just sat there with a stunned look on their face.

They started walking out of the auditorium in silence, with their heads hanging low.

Mom and Dad were really quiet on the way home, too.

So I know I finally did it.

I'm going to flunk my history class, for sure.

Who knows, I might even get kicked out of school.

80

But, all I know is that I can say goodbye to camp.

It's going to be the best summer ever!

Tuesday

I think I'm cursed.

No matter what I try, I can't get out of going to camp!

I know someone, somewhere, talked to a witch who put a curse on me.

I bet it was big mouth Jeff.

Or maybe it was Mike Magma. He probably has a witch for a ghoulfriend and she put a big hex on me.

Whatever it is, nothing I try seems to work.

I thought for sure that my presentation would get everyone at school so mad that they would definitely flunk me out of school.

How could I know there would be reporters at the school yesterday?

And how could I know that someone would record it and put it on the Mob-net?

But there I am, on the front page of today's paper.

"Possible Zombie Missing Link Discovered by Genius Middle School Zombie Kid."

And the recording went viral, so everyone in the Overworld is talking about it.

The Principal even talked about making me the 7th grade valedictorian.

And, my parents were so proud, that they promised they would pay for me to go to camp every year for the rest of my school life.

83

I don't get it.

I mean, I just don't get it.

Wednesday

Today all of the guys were talking about their summer plans again.

Creepy started telling me about how excited he was that I get to go to camp for a whole three weeks.

"They're going to have a lot of team building games, and cool sports stuff," he said. "We can even bunk together. I hope you don't mind, but I hiss sometimes when I sleep."

I don't know how I feel about the last thing Creepy said.

I started feeling a little sad because I was going to miss most of my friends this summer.

Sally had already left last week on her summer vacation.

Her parents planned to take her on a world tour of all the Biomes.

"Man, it sure must be cool having rich parents," I thought.

I told Sally how depressed I was about going to camp.

"Don't worry about it, Zombie. You might just have a great time. When I went to camp, I thought I would hate it too. But I ended up making some of the best friends I've ever had," she said.

"What about the killer counselors and the rotten flesh eating nurses?" I asked.

"That's just your imagination talking," she said. "Besides, the only thing that could kill you at camp is the cafeteria food. Just make sure you pack lots of snacks."

I wasn't sure if she was joking when she said that last part or if she was serious.

I guess it will be fun writing letters to my friends over the summer. And I can always call them.

My Mom said that if I fill my summer with a lot to do, summer vacation will go by real quick, and I'll see my friends at school in no time.

So, I'd better get used to making a lot of lanyards and macaroni pictures.

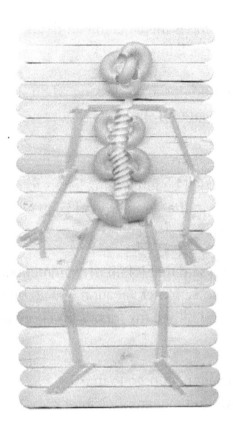

Thursday

We got our report cards today.

I never thought I would be sad about getting straight A's in all my classes, though.

Which is really weird because I've never gotten an A in any class. C's and D's are more my style.

I did get a B once. But I think it was because the gym teacher felt sorry for me.

I'm the Zombie that teachers always write on his report card, "He's got so much potential."

I figured that as long as the teachers know, why waste time trying to prove it?

Anyway, it feels really weird not having to hide my report card from my parents for a change.

No trying to erase my grade, or intercepting the teacher's zmail, or answering the phone using my Mom's voice.

I can actually just come home and hand my report card to my Mom and Dad.

Still feels really weird, though.

Today we had the 7th grade Mob award ceremony, too.

That's when all the 7th grade Mob kids get an award for not flunking out of Scare School, and making it to 8th grade.

For some reason, they made us wear these really funny caps and gowns.

Slimey had a hard time finding a cap and gown his size. So he used a piano cover instead.

Creepy had a hard time putting his on. I think it's because he doesn't have any arms.

You know, that's probably why he walks around naked all the time.

Skelee looked real good in his cap and gown. He said he didn't even have to buy one. His uncle had his old one lying around in the closet.

Though we still don't know what the sickle is for.

But we all got cool awards.

Slimey got the "Most Well-Rounded Student" award.

Creepy got the "Most Sensitive Student" award. I think that meant that he was sent home the most this school year.

Skelee got the "Most Transparent Student" award.

And I got the "Most Shocking Turnaround of Any Student, Ever" award.

Didn't really understand what that meant, but it was cool.

Friday

Today is our last day of school.

They decided to have a carnival for us, which I thought was really cool.

There's going to be rides, mob game booths, rotten candy, zombie clowns (which are really creepy by the way), a Scary-Go-Round, and a Ferris wheel.

Me and Skelee really like the Scary-Go-Round.

Slimey likes the rotten candy.

Creepy says he likes the Ferris wheel. He says he just loves the thrill of being up so high.

Sometimes I really don't understand what Creepy says... Everybody knows he's afraid of heights.

But, even though I have to go to camp in a few weeks, I'm looking forward to having fun these last few days of freedom with my friends.

Friday Night
Special Entry

The carnival was a lot of fun.

But the craziest thing happened toward the end of the night.

Me and Skelee decided to go on the Scary-Go-Round one last time.

I told Slimey to stick with Creepy so that Creepy wouldn't have to go on the Ferris wheel by himself.

But something happened.

Slimey must've gotten distracted by the rotten candy machine, because somehow he lost Creepy.

Next thing we know, there was a lot of screaming and yelling coming from the Ferris wheel.

We ran over there, and saw a big crowd.

Somehow the Ferris wheel got stuck, and there were Mob kids stuck in the seats.

I didn't want to look up… But I did.

And there was Creepy all the way at the top, all by himself.

I could tell he was scared, which meant trouble for everybody.

I went to the Enderman that was operating the ride.

"Hey, somebody needs to climb up there to get him down!" I said.

"Naw man, I just work here, bro," he said.

"Uuuurrrgghhh! Teenagers!" I thought.

I realized that if I climbed up there, I wouldn't be able to climb down with Creepy.

So I decided to climb up there and see if I could calm Creepy down.

So I climbed all the way to the top, which was really scary.

"Hey Creepy," I said. "How are you doing, buddy?"

"I'm really scared, Zombie. I want my Mom."

"Don't worry buddy, I'm here. I won't leave you alone," I said.

I tried to take his mind off of being up so high, so I talked to him about camp.

"I can't wait to go to camp with you, Creepy," I said. "We're going to have so much fun. We're going to make lanyards and macaroni pictures. We're going to do a lot of team building exercises. And we can bunk together in the same cabin. Camp is going to be a lot of fun, isn't it?"

"To be honest, Zombie, I really don't like camp," Creepy said.

"Really?"

"Yeah. I feel so lonely there. And all the kids just pick on me all the time. I think it's because I'm really bad at all of the sports and stuff. And I'm going to miss my Mom and Dad so much. And I'm really going to miss you and the guys a lot, too."

"Wow, Creepy. I didn't know," I said.

"But now that I know you're going, Zombie, it's going to be so much more fun," Creepy said, and he started smiling and stopped hissing.

Then, all of a sudden the Ferris wheel started moving again.

We got off the Ferris wheel and a Mobulance was waiting there for me and Creepy.

The Mobulance nurse put a blanket around Creepy and me and gave us some cake.

She was really nice.

"Thank you," we said.

"You're welcome. That was really brave of you to go up there and help your friend. I wish there were more kids like you around," she said.

"Hey, I know you!" Creepy said. "You're the nurse that works at our camp every summer."

"Creepy, right?" she said.

Creepy started turning red and green. I think he had a crush on her or something.

"Wow, you're the camp nurse?" I asked.

"Yep. I've worked at camp every year for the past few years," she said.

I wanted to ask her if she had a craving for rotten flesh, but she walked away to take care of the other mob kids.

"She remembered my name!" Creepy said.

Saturday

I went to go visit Steve today to tell him about all that happened at the carnival.

"Wow, Zombie," he said, "That was really cool. You really went out on a limb for Creepy."

"But I have all my limbs."

"No, I mean that you really came through for Creepy when he needed a friend," Steve said.

"Yeah. And you know, even though I don't want to go to camp, I think I'm going to go just so that Creepy can have a friend around. He said he gets real lonely at camp."

"Who's going to be there for you?" Steve said.

"I guess it doesn't matter… It's only for a few weeks anyway," I said.

"Well, it matters to me," Steve said. "That's why I'm going with you."

"Are you serious?"

"Hey, that's what friends are for," Steve said. "Besides, we can always sneak out and bother some witches or something."

Wow. Steve is like the best friend I've ever had.

Which is weird because he's human.

But I guess it doesn't matter if you're a human, Slime, Skeleton, or Creeper. All that matters is a true friend will always be there when you need them.

So, I'm going to camp in a few weeks.

But I'm not going alone. I'm going with two of the best friends any Zombie could ask for.

Plus, we're going to need all the help we can get if we're going to survive against the brain-eating, killer counselors...

And the cafeteria food monster...

Find out What Happens Next in...

Diary of a Minecraft Zombie Book 6
"Zombie Goes To Camp"

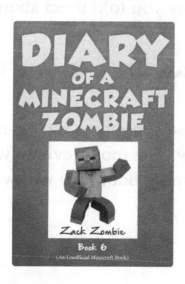

Get Your Copy and Join Zombie on More Exciting Adventures!

If you really liked this book, please tell a friend. I'm sure they will be happy you told them about it.

Leave Us a Review Too

Please support us by leaving a review. The more reviews we get the more books we will write!

Check Out All of Our Books in the Diary of a Minecraft Zombie Series

The Diary of a Minecraft Zombie Book 1
"A Scare of a Dare"

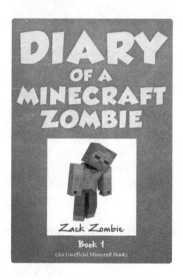

In the first book of this hilarious Minecraft adventure series, take a peek in the diary of an actual 12 year old Minecraft Zombie and all the trouble he gets into in middle school.

Get Your Copy Today!

The Diary of a Minecraft Zombie Book 2
"Bullies and Buddies"

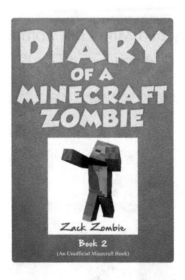

This time Zombie is up against some of the meanest and scariest mob bullies at school. Will he be able to stop the mob bullies from terrorizing him and his friends, and make it back in one piece?

Jump into the Adventure and Find Out!

The Diary of a Minecraft Zombie Book 3
"When Nature Calls"

What does a Zombie do for Spring break?
Find out in this next installment of the exciting
and hilarious adventures of a 12 year old
Minecraft Zombie!

Get Your Copy Today!

The Diary of a Minecraft Zombie Book 4
"Zombie Swap"

12 Year Old Zombie and Steve
have Switched Bodies!
Find out what happens as 12 year old
Zombie has to pretend to be human and
Steve pretends to be a zombie.

Jump into this Zany
Adventure Today!

The Diary of a Minecraft Zombie Book 5
"School Daze"

Summer Vacation is Almost Here and
12 Year Old Zombie Just Can't Wait!
Join Zombie on a Hilarious Adventure as
he tries to make it through the last few
weeks before Summer Break.

Jump into the
Adventure Today!

The Diary of a Minecraft Zombie Book 6
"Zombie Goes To Camp"

Join 12 year old Zombie, as he faces his
biggest fears, and tries to survive the next
3 weeks at Creepaway Camp.
Will he make it back in one piece?

Jump into His Crazy Summer Adventure and Find Out!

The Diary of a Minecraft Zombie Book 7
"Zombie Family Reunion"

Join Zombie and his family on their crazy
adventure as they face multiple challenges
trying to get to their 100th Year
Zombie Family Reunion.
Will Zombie even make it?

Get Your Copy Today
and Find Out!

The Diary of a Minecraft Zombie Book 8
"Back to Scare School"

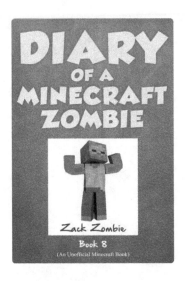

Zombie finally made it through 7th grade...
And he even made it through one really crazy
summer! But will Zombie be able to survive
through the first weeks of being an 8th grader
in Mob Scare School?

Find Out in His Latest
Adventure Today!

The Diary of a Minecraft Zombie Book 9
"Zombie's Birthday Apocalypse"

It's Halloween and it's Zombie's Birthday!
But there's a Zombie Apocalypse happening that
may totally ruin his Birthday party.Will Zombie
and his friends be able to stop the Zombie
Apocalypse so that they can finally enjoy some
cake and cookies at Zombie's Birthday Bash?

Jump into the Adventure
and Find Out!

The Diary of a Minecraft Zombie Book 10
"One Bad Apple"

There's a new kid at Zombie's middle school and everyone thinks he is so cool. But the more Zombie hangs out with him, the more trouble he gets into. Is this new Mob kid as cool as everyone thinks he is, or is he really a Minecraft Wolf in Sheep's clothing?

Jump Into this Zany Minecraft Adventure and Find Out!

CPSIA information can be obtained
at www.ICGtesting.com
Printed in the USA
BVHW020913131222
654113BV00003B/102